Explore Mars

Jackie Golusky

Lerner Publications ◆ Minneapolis

PAGE PLUS +

Scan the QR code on page 21 to see Mars in 3D!

Lerner Publications Company
An imprint of Lerner Publishing Group, Inc.
241 First Avenue North
Minneapolis, MN 55401 USA

For reading levels and more information, look up this title at www.lernerbooks.com.

Main body text set in Billy Infant regular.
Typeface provided by SparkType.

Library of Congress Cataloging-in-Publication Data

Names: Golusky, Jackie, 1996- author.
Title: Explore Mars / Jackie Golusky.
Other titles: Lightning bolt books. Planet explorer.
Description: Minneapolis, MN : Lerner Publications, 2021 | Series: Lightning bolt books - Planet explorer | Includes bibliographical references and index. | Audience: Ages 6-9 | Audience: Grades 2-3 | Summary: "Beginning readers get a close-up look at the coolest facts and science about Mars. The latest scientific discoveries and space missions are discussed in this accessible and energetic text"— Provided by publisher.
Identifiers: LCCN 2020014675 (print) | LCCN 2020014676 (ebook) | ISBN 9781728404103 (library binding) | ISBN 9781728423623 (paperback) | ISBN 9781728418469 (ebook)
Subjects: LCSH: Mars (Planet)—Juvenile literature.
Classification: LCC QB641 .G673 2021 (print) | LCC QB641 (ebook) | DDC 523.43—dc23

LC record available at https://lccn.loc.gov/2020014675
LC ebook record available at https://lccn.loc.gov/2020014676

Manufactured in the United States of America
1-48468-48982-6/15/2020

Table of Contents

All about Mars   4

Mars's Moons   10

Living on Mars   12

Checking Out Mars   16

Planet Facts   20

Space Story   21

Glossary   22

Learn More   23

Index   24

All about Mars

About 140 million miles (225 million km) away from Earth is a red, rocky planet called Mars.

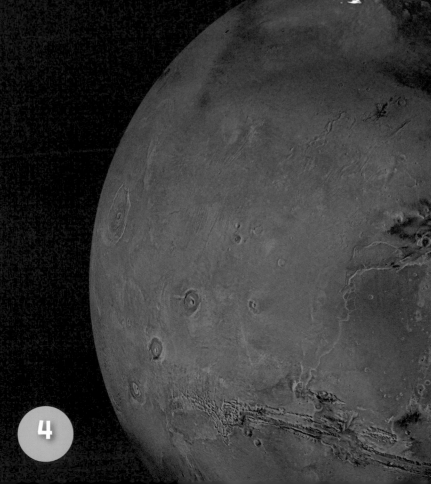

Mercury Venus Earth Mars Jupiter Saturn Uranus Neptune

This diagram shows the order of the planets in the solar system.

At 1.5 astronomical units (AU), Mars is the fourth planet from the sun. One AU is 93 million miles (150 million km), about the same distance from the sun to Earth.

Mars is made up of metal and rock. Its reddish color comes from the iron and oxygen in its dirt. Over time, the iron rusts because of the oxygen.

NASA's *Curiosity* rover takes a photo showing off Mars's red soil.

Mars has a radius of 2,106 miles (3,390 km), while Earth's radius is 3,959 miles (6,371 km). That means that Mars is about half as wide as Earth.

Mars and Earth (*left*) shown to scale

Mars's orbit is an oval around the sun. Its orbit can bring it close to Earth, making it appear very bright in the night sky.

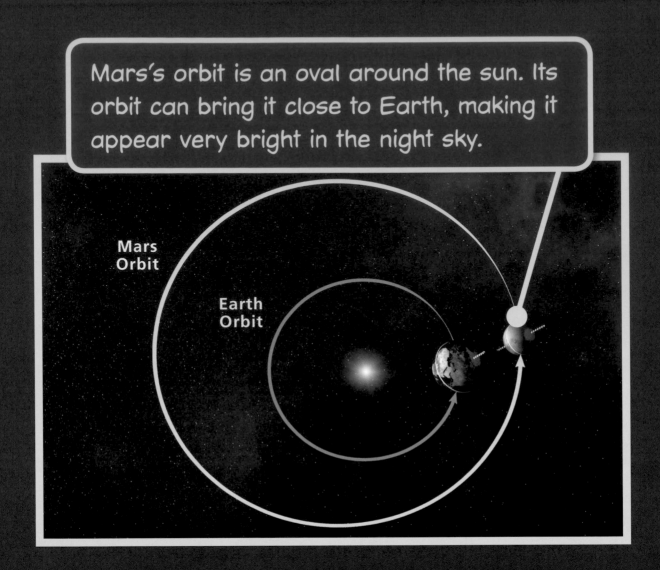

Mars orbits the sun in an oval-shaped path. Mars takes 687 Earth days to complete one orbit. This is nearly twice as long as Earth takes.

Atmosphere is a layer of gas surrounding a planet. Mars's atmosphere is very thin. It doesn't hold heat well. Mars can get as cold as −225°F (−143°C).

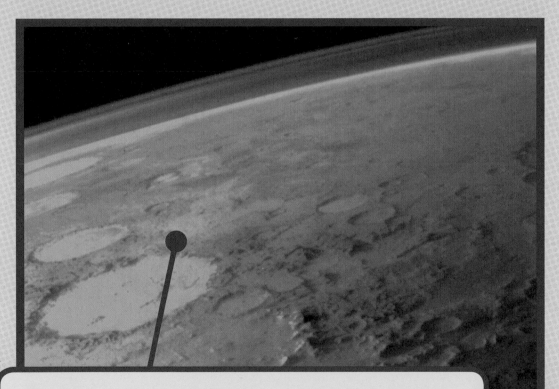

Mars's atmosphere is not made of the same materials as Earth's. You would not be able to breathe Mars's air.

Mars's Moons

Phobos and Deimos are Mars's two moons. They are shaped like potatoes and are among the smallest moons in the solar system.

Phobos is about two times the size of Deimos and has a lot of craters. Deimos is smoother and has a lot of dirt.

This image shows a spacecraft that NASA and Japan want to send to study Phobos and Deimos.

Living on Mars

Like Earth, Mars is tilted on an axis. This tilt gives Mars its seasons. In the summer, powerful dust storms can reach speeds of up to 66 miles (106 km) per hour. These storms can last for months.

This diagram shows how when autumn begins on Mars, Earth has already experienced autumn and some of winter.

Because Mars takes more time to orbit the sun, its seasons are longer than Earth's. Each season on Earth is about 90 days, while Mars's shortest season is about 142 days.

Mars's surface is covered with volcanoes, mountains, and canyons. The planet has the largest volcano in our solar system. This volcano, Olympus Mons, is three times taller than Mount Everest.

Some scientists think the most recent time that Olympus Mons erupted was two million years ago.

Bacolor Crater is located on the northern half of Mars. At about 12 miles (20 km) wide, it is larger than Washington, DC!

Mars has more than 635,000 impact craters. The craters were created by meteors hitting the planet.

Checking Out Mars

After Earth, Mars is the most explored planet in the solar system. Six spacecraft orbit Mars, and three spacecraft roam its surface.

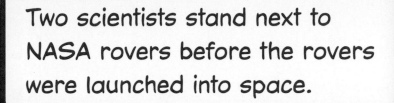

Two scientists stand next to NASA rovers before the rovers were launched into space.

Scientists believe that Mars could have liquid water. In 2003, NASA launched two rovers to Mars to find out. If there is liquid water on Mars, the planet might be able to support life.

Perseverance is a rover that is studying Mars. It launched in 2020 and is collecting samples of dirt and soil to learn more about the planet.

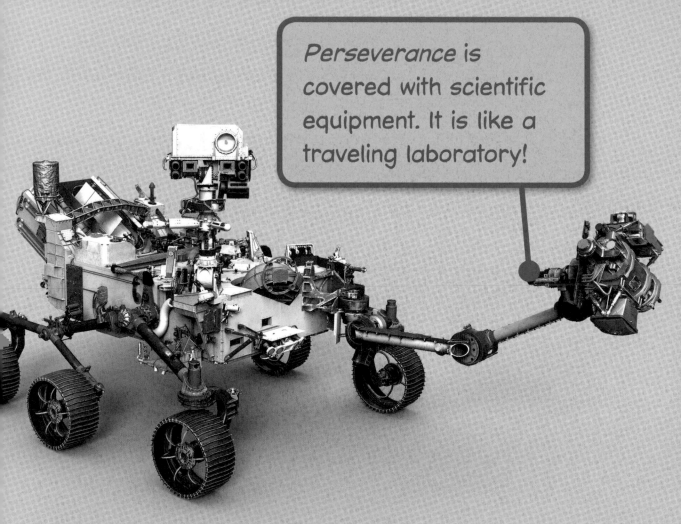

Perseverance is covered with scientific equipment. It is like a traveling laboratory!

One day, astronauts might walk on Mars.

Astronomers continue to learn more about Earth's neighbor planet, Mars.

Planet Facts

- Mars's atmosphere is one hundred times thinner than Earth's atmosphere.

- Mars has dry, riverlike channels that look as if they once had water.

- The planet is named after the Roman god of war.

Space Story

Mars can be seen without a telescope. People have been studying Mars for over four thousand years. Ancient Egyptians tracked the planet's movements across the sky. They called Mars Har Decher, meaning "the red one." They also looked at Mercury, Venus, Jupiter, and Saturn. The Babylonians, ancient Greeks, and Romans also studied Mars.

Scan the QR code to the right to see Mars in 3D!

Glossary

astronomical unit (AU): the distance between the sun and Earth

atmosphere: layer of gas around a planet

axis: an imaginary line running through an object around which the object rotates

crater: a large, round hole created by a meteor

meteor: a piece of rock flying through outer space

orbit: a path that one object follows as it travels around another

radius: half the distance across a circle

rover: a machine that explores the surface of another planet

Learn More

Golusky, Jackie. *Explore Earth*. Minneapolis: Lerner Publications, 2021.

Lawrence, Ellen. *Living on Mars*. New York: Bearport, 2019.

NASA Space Place: All about Mars
https://spaceplace.nasa.gov/all-about-mars/en/

NASA Space Place: Explore Mars—A Mars Rover Game
https://spaceplace.nasa.gov/explore-mars/en/

NASA Space Place: The Mars Rovers
https://spaceplace.nasa.gov/mars-rovers/en/

Sommer, Nathan. *Mars*. Minneapolis: Bellwether Media, 2019.

Index

atmosphere, 9

dust storms, 12

Olympus Mons, 14

Perseverance, 18

rovers, 17–18
rust, 6

seasons, 12–13

water, 17

Photo Acknowledgments

Image credits: NASA/JPL/USGS, p. 4; WP/Wikimedia Commons (CC BY-SA 3.0), p. 5; NASA/JPL-Caltech/MSSS, p. 6; NASA/JPL, p. 7; NASA, pp. 8, 9, 10, 13; JAXA/NASA, p. 11; NASA/JPL-Caltech/University of Arizona, p. 12; ESA/DLR/FU Berlin/J. Cowart (CC BY-SA 3.0 IGO), p. 14; NASA/JPL-Caltech/ASU, p. 15; JPL/NASA/ESA, p. 16; NASA/JPL/Thomas "Dutch" Slager, p. 17; NASA/JPL-Caltech, p. 18; NASA/JSC by Pat Rawlings (SAIC), p. 19.

Cover: NASA/JPL-Caltech.